Athletic Association. Princeton University.

Athletic Organizations of Princeton University

Their Histories, Records and Constitutions, June 1891

Athletic Association. Princeton University.

Athletic Organizations of Princeton University
Their Histories, Records and Constitutions, June 1891

ISBN/EAN: 9783337170561

Printed in Europe, USA, Canada, Australia, Japan

Cover: Foto ©ninafisch / pixelio.de

More available books at **www.hansebooks.com**

THE

Athletic Organizations

OF

Princeton University

———

THEIR HISTORIES, RECORDS AND CONSTITUTIONS

———

JUNE, 1891

The Princeton Press'

PREFACE.

Every Princeton student, by virtue of his membership in the College, is a member of each of the University Athletic Organizations, viz.: Foot Ball, Base Ball and Track Athletic. Each of these associations has three Directors, a President from the Senior Class, a Treasurer from the Junior Class, both elected by the College in mass meeting held for the purpose, and a Captain, chosen by the team of the previous year. These Directors carry on the business of their respective associations and have full control in their own organization. The Directors of the three associations, together with the University Treasurer, who is elected from the Senior Class by the College, constitute the Executive Committee, which has charge of the general interests of these associations and entire supervision of the University Field.

There is also an Advisory Committee of five graduates, chosen by the Executive Committee, subject to the ratification of the College, whose powers are mainly advisory, but who have the power of veto in the election of Captains and in permanent changes proposed for the Athletic grounds or buildings.

The Graduate Advisory Committee and the Executive Committee together form the University Athletic Association, which takes charge of the University Athletic funds and determines other matters of management which affect the organizations alike. It is the highest power in the College Athletic management.

Besides the University organizations there are several organizations—such as the Lacrosse Association, the Tennis Association, etc.—in which the membership is limited, and which are largely independent both of the Executive Committee and the University Athletic Association. The test of membership in the University Association is the ability of an association to form a team which can fairly represent the College in the Intercollegiate Championship series. Thus Lacrosse was dropped from the University Association in 1890, because, in the opinion of the best players, a representative team could not be put in the field in 1891.

These associations have all the privileges of the University Field at hours fixed by the Executive Committee. They are also in communication with the Graduate Advisory Committee on the same basis as the other associations.

The Faculty supervision of Athletics is entrusted to the Out-door Sports Committee. This Committee, besides a general interest in the conduct of Athletics, have control of all questions in which Athletics affect the general instruction and morale of the College or the personnel of the teams. They therefore exercise supervision of all the schedules for games, and the appointment of trainers, etc., must have their approval.

The present organization and management was practically initiated in March, 1888, by the adoption of the greater part of the present constitutions and institution of the Executive Committee. Previous to that every association was independent and worked solely for its own interests, and it was generally admitted that the very poor showing made in all branches of Athletics between 1886 and 1888 was due to poor management. Since the organization of the Executive Committee has brought the officers of all the associations and of the Advisory Committee together, a thoroughly University spirit has sprung up of coöperation between the associations and committees both of undergraduates and alumni, leading to the recent formation of the University Athletic Association.

Histories and Records.

FOOT BALL.

The first authentic information of Foot Ball being played in Princeton is found in the College records of 1858, when various clubs and associations were formed, and among these a regular foot ball club of unlimited numbers. It was not until 1864 that another club was formed. The popularity of the game, however, was of slow growth until 1868. The following year, 1869, Princeton organized and sent a team of twenty-five men to New Brunswick, and was defeated in her first match game by Rutgers, by a score of 6 goals to 4. But two weeks later Princeton had her turn by defeating Rutgers 8 goals to 0. In 1870 Rutgers was once more defeated, and, refusing to play the following year, the games were again confined to Princeton's own class and club teams.

In 1872 Princeton challenged Columbia, Yale and Rutgers. Yale's faculty refused to allow the team to play outside of New Haven. Columbia declined. Rutgers accepted and was defeated. The game had now become more popular, and in 1873 the first Inter-Collegiate Foot Ball Convention was held in New York, at which Yale, Rutgers and Princeton were represented. Playing rules were adopted and the teams were reduced to twenty men. This year Princeton met Yale for the first time and defeated her on her own grounds by 3 goals to 0.

In 1876 Princeton followed the example of Harvard and Yale and adopted the Rugby game. She challenged Yale to a game on Thanksgiving Day. Yale accepted, and Princeton received her first defeat since 1869.

In the fall of '77, at a call from Princeton, a convention was held at Springfield, Mass., and the Inter-Collegiate Foot Ball Association was formed, consisting of Harvard, Columbia and Princeton. In the spring of this year Harvard had defeated Princeton in a practice game, but after the formation of the Association Princeton defeated both Harvard and Columbia, and thus won the championship of 1877. Yale had refused to enter the League, and did not play Harvard or Columbia, but accepted a challenge from Princeton, and a game was played on December 8th, which resulted in a draw, both sides failing to score.

In '78 Princeton won the championship by defeating Columbia, Harvard and Yale.

In '79 the Yale-Harvard and Yale-Princeton games were drawn, but Princeton defeated Harvard and again won the championship.

In '80 the Yale-Princeton game was a tie, and Princeton still held the championship.

In '81 Yale won the championship and kept it in '82 and '83.

In the game between Yale and Princeton in '84 the score stood 6–4 in favor of Yale, when Moffat dropped a goal from the field, which the referee refused to allow on the ground that he was not watching the ball. The official score, therefore, stands 6–4 in favor of Yale; but no championship was awarded, as the game was unfinished on account of darkness.

Owing to faculty restrictions Harvard withdrew from the Association in 1885, and Princeton won the championship, defeating Yale on her own grounds by the close score of 6–5.

A new Association was formed in 1886, consisting of Yale, Harvard, Wesleyan, University of Pennsylvania and Princeton. No championship was awarded, as the deciding game between Yale and Princeton was again unfinished on account of darkness. The two years following Yale won the championship, but in '89 Princeton brought the championship back to Nassau by defeating Yale 10–0, and Harvard 41–15.

In 1890 Yale won the championship of the Association by defeating Princeton, but was in turn defeated by Harvard, who, owing to faculty restrictions, had again withdrawn from the Association and did not meet Princeton.

The following is Princeton's complete record in the championship series since the founding of the Inter-Collegiate Foot Ball Association in 1877:

1877.	GOALS.	TOUCH-DOWNS.		GOALS.	TOUCH-DOWNS.
Harvard	0	2	Princeton	1	1
Columbia	0	0	"	4	7
Yale	0	0	"	0	0

Yale not in Association, championship awarded to Princeton.

1878.	GOALS.	TOUCH-DOWNS.		GOALS.	TOUCH-DOWNS.
Columbia	..	..	Princeton	..	..
Harvard	0	0	"	0	1
Yale	0	0	"	1	0

Championship awarded to Princeton.

Safeties were introduced in this year, but were not counted in the scores.

1879.	GOALS.	TOUCH-DOWNS.	SAFETIES.		GOALS.	TOUCH-DOWNS.	SAFETIES.
Columbia.............	0	0	10	Princeton........	2	3	0
Harvard.................	0	0	5	"	1	0	7
Yale.....................	0	0	2	"	1	0	5

Yale-Harvard game a tie. Princeton by defeating Harvard won championship.

1880.

Columbia..........forfeited to				Princeton			
Harvard.................	1	1	4	"	2	2	6
Yale	0	0	5	"	1	0	11

Princeton still held championship.

1881.

Columbia.............	0	0	4	Princeton............	1	2	1
Harvard.................	0	0	1	"	0	0	1
Yale	0	0	0	"	0	0	0

Yale defeated Harvard, thus winning championship.

1882

Harvard.................	1	1	0	Princeton............	1	0	2
Columbia........	0	0	0	"	3	1	0
Yale	2	0	1	"	1	0	1

Championship awarded to Yale.

Scoring by points introduced this year.

Goal from Touch-down ....6 points.

     "   Field....................5 "

     Touchdown 4   "

     Safety by opponents..........................2   "

1883.	POINTS.			POINTS.
Columbia..........forfeited to		Princeton........................		
Harvard..............................	7	"		26
Yale	6	"		0

Championship awarded to Yale.

1884.

| Harvard.. | 6 | Princeton | 34 |
| Yale | 6 | " | 4 |

Yale-Princeton game unfinished on account of darkness, and no championship was awarded.

1885.

Wesleyan	0	Princeton	76
Yale	5	"	6
Univ. of Penn	0	"	51

Championship awarded to Princeton.

1886.

Univ. of Penn	6	Princeton	28
Harvard	0	"	12
Wesleyan	6	"	76
Yale	4	"	0

Yale-Princeton game unfinished on account of darkness, and no championship was awarded.

1887.

Wesleyan	0	Princeton	69
Univ. of Penn	0	"	95
Harvard	12	"	0
Yale	12	"	0

Championship awarded to Yale.

1888.

Wesleyan	0	Princeton	44
Univ. of Penn	0	"	4
Harvard	6	"	18
Yale	10	"	0

Championship awarded to Yale.

1889.

Univ. of Penn	4	Princeton	72
Wesleyan	0	"	98
Harvard	15	"	41
Yale	0	"	10

Championship awarded to Princeton.

1890.

Univ of Penn	0	Princeton	6
Wesleyan	4	"	46
Yale	32	"	0

Yale won the championship of the Association, but was defeated by Harvard, who was not in the Asssociation and did not play Princeton.

BASE BALL.

In looking over the records we find that base ball, like foot ball, was a favorite sport away back in the fifties; 1858 seems to have been a great year for the development of sport at Princeton; for, as in foot ball, so in base ball, we find the first record of the organization of a team in that year. It was a Freshman team, the first in Princeton's history. From the start the new sport met with favor; other classes tried the game; boarding clubs and halls soon followed, and, springing from the general movement, the next season saw a College nine, the Nassaus (that was in 1859). For four years the teams played with the clubs of neighboring cities or sought glory in defeating minor college nines.

In the fall of 1864 Williams College sent out a base ball team, and from them Princeton won her first college game, 27 to 16. The next year we lost to Williams on their grounds by a score of 30 to 17; in '66 Rutgers was defeated by 40 runs to 2.

In 1867 a class team from Princeton played two games with a Yale team, winning at Princeton by a score of 58 to 2, and at New Haven by 19 runs to 18.

The game was placed on a firmer footing when, in 1869, the Princeton University Base Ball Association was organized. Between 1869 and 1879 Princeton played games with various college teams.

The records with Yale and Harvard are as follows: In the matches with Harvard Princeton won 3 to her adversary's 8. Yale won 9 to Princeton's 4.

Under the original Inter-Collegiate Association Princeton's standing among the colleges was as follows:

	1880. W. L.	1881. W. L.	1882. W. L.	1883 W. L.	1884. W. L.	1885. W. L.	1886. W. L.	Total W. L.	Percentage Won.
Yale		7–3	8–3	7–1	9–2	7–3	9 2	47–14	.754
Harvard...	3–5	6–4	5–5	2–6	8–3	10–0	8–3	42–26	.617
Princeton	6–2	6..4	7–4	6–2	2–8	7–3	7–3	41–26	.612
Dartm'th.	4–4	4–6	3–7	....	1–9	4–6	....	16–32	.333
Brown......	5–3	4–6	4–6	1–7	5–5	1–9	2–8	22–44	.318
Amherst..	2–6	3–7	4–6	4–4	6–4	1–9	1–9	21–45	.303
Williams.							4–6	4–6	.400

A decided change was made in the college base ball arena in 1887. Yale, Harvard and Princeton withdrew from the Inter-Collegiate Association and organized as the Eastern College League.

In 1887 Yale won easily, the record being:

Year of 1887.	Yale.	Harvard.	Princeton	Games Won.	Per Cent of Victories.
Yale		3	4	7	.87
Harvard.....................	1		2	3	.428
Princeton	0	1		1	.143
Games lost...............	1	4	6		

In the following year Yale retained the championship, with Harvard a close second.

Year of 1888.	Yale.	Harvard.	Princeton.	Games Won	Per Cent. of Victories.
Yale		3	3	6	.750
Harvard.....................	1		4	5	.625
Princeton	1	0		1	.125
Games lost...............	2	3	7		

The last season of the Tri-College League, 1889,
proved to be very interesting. The season opened on
May 4th, and on May 30th Yale and Princeton were tied
for first place, with Harvard a sure third. In June Princeton fell off in playing and Yale took the race.

YEAR OF 1889.	YALE.	PRINCETON.	HARVARD.	GAMES WON	PER CENT. OF VICTORIES.
Yale.............................		3	4	7	.875
Princeton...............	1	...	2	3	.375
Harvard...............	0	2	...	2	.250
Games lost...............	1	5	6	...	......

In 1890 no games were played with Harvard. The
four games with Yale were remarkable for closeness of
scores, fine playing and large attendance.

YEAR OF 1890.	AT NEW HAVEN, May 3d.	AT PRINCETON, May 24.	AT NEW YORE, June 14th.	AT BROOKLYN, June 18th.	GAMES WON.	PER CENT. OF VICTORIES.
Yale.............................	3	0	8	6	2	666
Princeton...............	2	1	8	5	1	.333

TRACK ATHLETICS.

The Princeton Athletic Club was organized in the early spring of 1873. Delegates were appointed from each of the three upper classes, who made arrangements for the first field meeting. This meeting was held on the University ball grounds on June 21, 1873. The rules by which the games were regulated were rules usually observed in the Scottish games of America, Mr. Goldie being at once the expounder and referee.

For two years the Caledonian games were thus conducted when the club determined to strengthen itself by a formal and independent organization. Accordingly, after January 26, 1876, the club possessed a constitution and a series of officers. An Executive Committee was also appointed to regulate the games, and in conjunction with the Professor of Gymnastics to select representatives for the Inter-Collegiate contests. A forward step was also taken in the establishment of two yearly Field meetings. For a time this innovation did not succeed, the interest being centered in the established Commencement games. Then only were prizes awarded, and then only was established the reputation of the best general athlete of the year. For this reason we have taken notice in the following tables only of the Commencement games. The graduated records here given will indicate the progress made from year to year:

COLLEGE GAMES.—I. *Leaping.*

[A dash signifies omission of the game; dotted lines, that the records were poorer than the preceding.]

PRINCETON.	STANDING LONG JUMP.	RUNNING LONG.	STANDING HIGH.	RUNNING HIGH.	HOP, STEP AND JUMP.	HITCH AND KICK.	THREE JUMPS.
1873 June 21	S. R. Hutchinson, 10 ft. 2½ in.	J. T. Fredericks. 18 ft. 10 in.	G. C. Hendrickson 4 ft. 6 in.	A. Marquand 5 ft. 3 in.	G. C. Hendrickson 42 ft. 3 in.	G. C. Hendrickson 8 ft. 5 in.	—
1874 June 20	....	L. G. Walker 18 ft. 10¾ in. / S. R. Hutchinson 18 ft. 10½ in.	....	....	....	....	—
1875 June 26	....	....		T. Sheldon 5 ft. 6 in. / J. H. Lionberger. 5 ft. 5 in. (Somersaults).	....		—
1876 June 21	....	L. G. Walker 19 ft.		A. J. McCosh 5 ft. 3 in.			—
1877 June 18	....	H. Stevenson 19 ft. 3 in.	F. Larkin 4 ft. 8 in.	A. J. McCosh 5 ft. 5 in.			—
1878 June 17	—	A. C. Hunt 20 ft.	....	....			F. Larkin 32 ft. 4 in.

COLLEGE GAMES.—II. *Running and Walking.*

PRINCETON.	MILE RUN.	HALF MILE.	QUARTER MILE.	DASH.	THREE MILE WALK.	MILE WALK.	THREE-LEGGED RACE.
1873 June 21		J. H. Vandeventer 2 min. 15 sec.		S. B. Hutchinson (125 yards) 13 sec.			
1874 June 20			J. H. Vandeventer 1 min.	S. B. Hutchinson (100 yards) 9½ sec.			{ Hutchinson Cummings
1875 June 26	R. Greene 5 min. 25¾ sec.					B. Hall 8 min. 59 sec.	
1876 June 24	R. Greene 5 min. 15 2-5 sec.						{ Halstead A. J. McCosh 13½ sec.
1877 June 18	W. Bearns, Columbia. 5 min. 10 2-5 sec.		A. J. McCosh 54½ sec.				
1878 June 17		J. A. Stewart 2 min. 9¾ sec. M. S. Paton 2 min. 11 sec.		100 yards..... (220 yards) L. P. Smock 24 2-5 sec.			

College Games.—III. *Miscellaneous.*

PRINCETON.	HURDLE RACE.	PUTTING THE SHOT.	THROWING THE HAMMER.	VAULTING WITH POLE.	THROWING BASE BALL.	SACK-RACE.
1873 June 21	H. C. Beach (8 hurdles) 22 sec. 100 yds.	F. Biddle (16 lbs.) 32 ft. 10 in.	W. S. Cheesman (13 lbs.) 112 ft.	A. Marquand 8 ft. 1 in.	W. B Devereux 335 ft.	J. H. Lionberger.
1874 June 20	H. C. Beach (8 hurdles) 15 sec. 100 yds.	F. Biddle (16 lbs.) 33 ft. 3½ in.		....	J. M. Mann, 343 ft. 9 in.	
1875 June 26	J. M. Woods (10 hurdles) 19½ sec. 120 yds.	....	....	....	{ J. O. Denny, 358 ft. J. M. Woods, 351 ft.	
1876 June 24	J. M. Woods (10 hurdles) 19 1-5 sec. 120 yds.	....	....	{ A. J. McCosh 8 ft. 8 in. F. A. Marquand 8 ft. 6 in.	J.O. Denney, 375 ft. 9 in.	
1877 June 18	H. Stevenson 18½ sec. (10 hurdles) 120 yds.	....	....	....	J. M. Mann, 375 ft.	
1878 June 17	A. Brown 18 1-5 sec. (10 hurdles) 120 yds.	F. Larkin 33 ft. 8 in.				

BEST GENERAL ATHLETES.

1873. J. C. Hendrickson.
1874. J. C. Vandevener.
1875. S. B. Hutchinson.
1876. A. J. McCosh.
1877. A. J. McCosh.
1878. F. Larkin.

But Princeton's contests in athletic games have not been confined to the town of Princeton. Before the second annual games had been held she had begun to win for herself laurels from outside sources. The first of these contests, on November 8, 1873, seemed a peculiarily auspicious occasion for Princeton to test her athletic ability. It was entitled a National Amateur Gymnastic and Athletic Tournament, and was held in the Academy of Music, New York. Its name did not reveal the full extent of the enterprise. Literary efforts were to be stimulated as well as physical. It seemed as though a new Olympia was to be established upon American soil. The literary contest, however, was quite subsidiary to the other. It was limited to a practical essay upon physical culture, and the prize awarded to a well-known practical gymnast. The athletic and gymnastic exercises were arranged so as to exhibit a great variety of skill. Twenty-five gold medals were offered for the various contests, and diplomas for those who came out second. Amid the eighty representatives from thirteen gymnasiums and athletic clubs from New York, Boston, Yonkers, Staten Island and Chicago, the nine Princeton students were almost indistinguishable. But they had not come in vain. In the various contests in which they were entered they asserted their ability to cope with their adversaries, and at the end of the struggle it appeared that they had won fifteen first and second, beside several third prizes. They had gained also the greatest prize of the Tournament, the medal for the best general gymnast. It was this occasion which gave to T. Sheldon of the Class of 1875 the reputation which he afterwards so well sustained. The Tournament has never been repeated upon the national scale. It was too grand an ideal for those who had to execute it. The colleges have now through the Inter-Collegiate Association a more practical method of testing their athletic powers.

Inter-Collegiate Athletic games were first held at Saratoga, on the 17th of July, 1874. Following immediately as they did the annual regatta, in which nine colleges had participated, the attention of a large public was directed from college sports upon the water to these games upon the land. The programme was limited to various contests in running, walking and hurdle-racing, as few of the colleges had attempted other Caledonian games. Princeton was represented by two contestants, and carried off two of the handsome Bennett prizes, the second in the Mile Run, and the second in the Hurdle-Race. Similar games were held the year following, to which Princeton sent no representatives.

Another year and an Inter-Collegiate Athletic Association had been formed. This was an important step, securing for Athletic interests a continued existence after Inter-Collegiate regattas had ceased to be. The management of the games now passed out of the hands of the Regatta Committee into the control of the new and independent organization. A code of rules was drawn up for the regulation of the games, and the lists of contests extended so as to include jumping, throwing the base ball, putting the shot and a three-legged race. Two games for Graduates, a mile run and a mile walk, were also added to the list. Once again at Saratoga, and in the wake of the last General College Regatta, the athletic games were held, under the auspices of the new Association. There was a goodly array of contestants, but the six representatives from Princeton soon distinguished themselves by winning eight prizes—four firsts and four seconds—thus establishing for the College an inter-collegiate reputation in athletics which we had failed to secure in boating.

The games of the following year were held at Mott Haven, July 6th, under the hospitality of the New York Athletic Club. They consisted in running 100 yards, 220 yards, quarter-mile, half-mile, mile; 120 yards hurdle-race; in walking: one mile, two miles; in leaping, running broad and running high, in putting the shot, pole vaulting, and throwing the hammer; and for Graduates 100 yards dash and mile walk. The exclusion of contests in endurance, as the seven mile walk and the three mile run, and the introduction of a variety of Scotch games, are worthy of notice.

Besides winning the two Graduate races Princeton carried off three first and four second prizes. The records in these contests were good. Still better, however, were those of the last Inter-Collegiate Athletic contests at Mott Haven, May 18, 1878. The programme omitted none of the exercises of the preceding year, but added contests in standing high and standing broad jumping. The honors for Princeton were carried off in the main by F. Larkin, Class of 1879, who secured the first place in each of the four contests which he entered. Another first and two second complete the list of the Undergraduate prizes. Princeton also came off victorious in both of the Graduate games.

PRINCETON'S RECORDS AT INTER-COLLEGIATE GAMES.

YEAR.	FIRSTS.	SECONDS.	THIRDS.
1876	4	4	1
'77	3	4	2
'78	5	2	1½
'79	4	3	2½
'80	1		
'81	1	2	1
'82	2		1½
'83	2	3	1
'84	1	1	
'85		1	1
'86			2
'87		1	3
'88			1
'89	2	1	
'90	3	4	1

PRINCETON'S BEST RECORDS.

Standing Long Jump	10 ft. 2½ in.
Standing High Jump	4 ft. 8 in.
Hop, Step and Jump	42 ft. 3 in.
Three Jumps	32 ft. 4 in.
Three-legged Race	13½ seconds.
Throwing Hammer (13 lbs.)	112 ft.
Throwing Base Ball	375 ft. 9 in.
100 Yards Run	9½ seconds.
120 "	13 "
220 "	22 "
440 "	51 "
440 " (Freshman)	59 "
880 "	1 min. 59⅔ sec.

1 Mile Run . . . . 4 min. 40 sec.
220 Hurdle . . . . 80 sec.
1 Mile Walk . . . . 7 min. 17½ sec.
2 Mile Bicycle . . . . 6 min. 54 sec.
High Jump . . . . 5 ft. 10¼ in.
Broad Jump . . . . 21 ft. 4 in.
Pole Vault . . . . 10 ft. 6 in.
Throwing the Hammer (16 lbs.) . . . . 90 ft. 1 in.
Putting Short (16 lbs.) . . . . 39 ft. 5 in.

BEST INTER-COLLEGIATE RECORDS.

440 Yards Dash . . .   50 sec., W. C. Dohm, '90.
880   "   . . . 1 min. 57⅓ sec.   "   "   "

BEST COLLEGE RECORDS.

100 Yards Dash . . . . 10 sec., L. Cary, '93
880   "   . . 1 min. 55¼ sec., W. C. Dohm, '90.

LACROSSE.

Princeton's record in Lacrosse is one of which she may well be proud. In the eight years when she was a member of the Intercollegiate Lacrosse League, Princeton three times won the championship, once tied for first place, and always stood among the leading colleges.

The Intercollegiate Lacrosse League was formed in 1883; the colleges composing it were, Harvard, Yale, Columbia. University of New York, and Princeton. The championship this first year was a tie between Harvard, Yale and Princeton. Columbia having lost every game during the Season, withdrew from the League.

Princeton won the championship in '84, and after the close of the Season, Yale withdrew from the League. Harvard won the championship in '85.

In '86 Stevens was admitted to the League. Harvard again won the championship. Yale was not in the League, but put a team in the field and played a challenge game in Princeton, which resulted in a victory for Princeton, with a score of 5 to 0. This was the last game of Lacrosse between Yale and Princeton.

The Season of '87 resulted in a victory for Harvard. In '88, Princeton won the championship and in this year Lehigh was admitted to the League for the first time. In '89, Princeton again won the championship, defeating Harvard on her own grounds by a score of 3 to 1. After the close of the Season Harvard withdrew from the League. Johns Kopkins was admitted to the League in '90, and the Season resulted in the championship going to Lehigh.

Last Fall owing to lack of interest throughout the college, and their consequent inability to put a representative team in the field, the Lacrosse Association withdrew from the Intercollegiate League and from the College Executive Committee.

THE GRADUATE ADVISORY COMMITTEE.

TO SERVE UNTIL MARCH, 1893.

Chairman, HENRY F. OSBORN, '77,
Princeton.

TO SERVE UNTIL MARCH, 1894.

Treasurer, CORNELIUS C. CUYLER, '79,
52 William St., New York City.

TO SERVE UNTIL MARCH, 1893.

DUNCAN EDWARDS, '85,
5 Beekman St., New York City.

TO SERVE UNTIL MARCH, 1892.

TRACY H. HARRIS, '86,
137 Broadway, New York City.

TO SERVE UNTIL MARCH, 1893,

HENRY B. THOMPSON, '77,
Rockford, near Wilmington, Del.

GRADUATE TREASURER.

CORNELIUS C. CUYLER, '79.

THE EXECUTIVE COMMITTEE.

President,
GLENN F. McKINNEY, '91.

University Treasurer and Secretary,
JOHN H. SEALY, '91.

FOOT BALL.

President, MAX FARRAND, '92.
Treasurer, GEORGE C. FRASER, '93.
Captain, RALPH H. WARREN, '93.

BASE BALL.

President, GLENN F. McKINNEY, '91.
Treasurer, JAMES P. PARKER, '92.
Captain, CHARLES C. DANA, '91.

TRACK ATHLETICS.

President, WILLARD H. BRADFORD '91.
Treasurer, CROWLEY WENTWORTH, '92.
Captain, JOSEPH S. RODDY, '91.

Constitutions.

PRINCETON UNIVERSITY ATH-LETIC ASSOCIATION.

ARTICLE I.

This body shall be known as the Princeton University Athletic Association.

ARTICLE II.

The object of this Association shall be to regulate the general athletic interests of all the organizations; to take charge of the University athletic funds, and to determine other matters of management which affect the organizations alike.

ARTICLE III.

This Association shall consist of the members of the Graduate Advisory Committee and the Executive Committee.

ARTICLE IV.

SEC. I. The Chairman of the Graduate Advisory Committee shall preside at all the regular meetings of this Association, but at any special meeting, the Chairman of the Committee calling that meeting shall preside.

SEC. II. The University Treasurer shall be the Secretary and Treasurer of this Association.

Article V.

Sec. I. There shall be three regular meetings of this Association held in Princeton each year, ordinarily as follows, one on the first Saturday in October, one on the second Saturday in February, and one on the Saturday before Commencement.

Sec. II. At any meeting of this Association, the Graduate Advisory Committee and Executive Committee shall each have one vote determined by a majority of the members present of each Committee, and no business shall be transacted which does not receive the sanction of both Committees.

Article VI.

Sec. I. Of this Association there shall be a Finance Committee, consisting of three members of the Graduate Advisory Committee, to be chosen at the Spring meeting of that Committee, and the Presidents of the Foot Ball, Base Ball, and Track Athletic Associations.

Sec. II. It shall be the duty of this Committee to invest, so as to insure the greatest benefits to the athletic interests of the College, all money paid to them for that purpose by the Treasurers of the various organizations.

Sec. III. This Committee shall elect one of its Graduate members as Treasurer, who shall be known as the Graduate Treasurer. It shall be the duty of the Graduate Treasurer to take charge of the University Athletic funds and to dispose of them only at the direction of this Committee. He shall make a report to the University Athletic Association at each regular meeting.

GRADUATE ADVISORY COMMITTEE.

ARTICLE I.

This body shall be called the Graduate Advisory Committee of Princeton College.

ARTICLE II.

The object of the Committee shall be to promote the athletic interests of the College.

ARTICLE III.

SEC. I. Any Alumnus of the College or any one who has taken a four years' course in College, shall be eligible to membership on the Committee, at least one of whom shall have graduated within three years of the time of election.

SEC. II. In the election of the Committee special reference shall be paid to the abilities and qualifications of proposed membership, as advisors in foot ball, base ball, and track athletics. It is, moreover, desirable that at least one member of the Committee be a resident in or near Princeton.

ARTICLE IV.

SEC. I. The Committee shall consist of five members, all of whom shall be elected by the

Executive Committee, subject to the ratification of the College, at the regular Annual Foot Ball Meeting to be held on the first Wednesday in March, and shall hold office for three years.

Article V.

The officers of the Committee shall consist of a Chairman, and a Secretary and Treasurer.

Article VI.

Sec. I. It shall be the duty of the Chairman to preside at all meetings of the Committee, and to cast the deciding vote in case of a tie.

Sec. II. It shall be the duty of the Secretary and Treasurer to keep a record of the proceedings of the meetings and to preside in the absence of the Chairman. He shall, moreover, take charge of all moneys collected by the Committee from the alumni for the benefit of athletics in College, and pay out the same according to the directions of the Committee.

Sec. III. The Secretary and Treasurer shall also inspect the accounts of the Treasurers of the various athletic organizations, represented in the Executive Committee, as presented by the University Treasurer, at each regular meeting of the University Athletic Association.

Article VII.

Sec. I. All officers of the Committee shall be elected by a majority vote of the Committee.

Sec. II. The Chairman shall be elected for a term of one year.

Article VIII.

Sec. I. There shall be three regular meetings of this Committee, held in Princeton, each year, ordinarily as follows, one on the first Saturday in October, one on the second Saturday in February, and one on the Saturday before Commencement.

Sec. II. At the regular Spring meeting of this Committee, three members shall be chosen, to serve on the Finance Committee of University Athletic Association.

Article IX.

Sec. I. The Advisory Committee shall be consulted in regard to all matters of importance, which pertain to the athletic welfare of the College, such as business of conventions, schedules of games, trainers, etc.

Sec. II. When a new Captain shall be elected by any athletic team of the College, his election shall not be valid until ratified by the Advisory Committee, who shall take action upon the election within three weeks, and if the Advisory Committee veto his election, another must be chosen in his place.

SEC. III. If satisfactory evidence shall be produced to show that an officer of any athletic organization of the College is guilty of maladministration or be incompetent, the Committee shall be empowered to demand the resignation of said officer and order the election of a successor, by the body accustomed to elect such officers.

SEC. IV. In regard to any changes contemplated by the officers of any athletic organization which shall involve additions to or alteration in the athletic grounds or buildings of the College, of such a nature as to permanently affect the interests of any or all the various athletic organizations, the Advisory Committee must first be consulted and shall have the power of veto.

EXECUTIVE COMMITTEE.

Article I.

Sec. I. This body shall be called the Executive Athletic Committee of Princeton College.

Article II.

Sec. I. The object of this Committee shall be to promote the general athletic interests of the College.

Article III.

Sec. I. This Committee shall consist of the Senior and Junior officers of the Foot Ball Association, Base Ball Association, Track Athletic Association and the University Treasurer.

Sec. II. The officers of the Committee shall consist of a Chairman, and a Secretary and Treasurer.

Sec. III. The Chairman shall be elected by a majority vote of the Committee, at the first meeting in first term.

Sec. IV. The University Treasurer shall be the Secretary and Treasurer of the Executive Committee.

Article IV.

Sec. I. It shall be the duty of the Chairman to call special meetings of the Committee at the request of the Foot Ball, Base Ball or Track Athletic Associations, or of the University Treasurer. The Chairman shall preside at all meetings and cast the deciding vote in case of a tie.

Sec. II. It shall be the duty of the Secretary and Treasurer to keep a record of the proceedings of the meetings held by the Committee, and of all College mass meetings held for athletic purposes.

Article V.

Sec. I. There shall be a regular meeting of the Committee, on the second Monday of each month, during the College year, time and place to be fixed by the Chairman.

Sec. II. Five members of the Committee shall constitute a quorum, and each Association must be represented in the quorum.

Sec. III. Every member of the Committee shall have a vote. The Chairman shall vote only in case of a tie.

Sec. IV. It shall take a two-thirds vote of members of the College assembled in mass meeting to make void any action of the Executive Committee.

ARTICLE VI.

SEC. I. There shall be a University Treasurer elected from the Junior Class by a majority vote of the undergraduates present at the regular Annual Base Ball Meeting held the last Thursday in May.

SEC. II. It shall be the duty of the University Treasurer to audit the accounts of the Treasurers of the various athletic organizations represented in the Executive Committee and submit a report of the same to the University Athletic Association, at each of their regular meetings.

SEC. III. It shall be the duty of the University Treasurer to collect from the Treasurers of the various Associations represented in the Executive Committee, money sufficient to defray the expenses of the Executive Committee. The amount which each Association shall pay, shall be decided by the Executive Committee.

SEC. IV. The University Treasurer shall exercise a general supervision of the University Athletic Field and Buildings, see to all necessary repairs and alterations and obtain authority for all larger expenditures from the Executive Committee. He shall also have special charge of the Grand Stand.

Sec. V. The University Treasurer shall be the Secretary and Treasurer of the University Athletic Association.

Sec. VI. The University Treasurer shall transact according to the directions of the Executive Committee all business, financial or otherwise, connected with the general athletic welfare of the various associations, not pertaining strictly to or falling under the jurisdiction of any one organization.

Sec. VII. The University Treasurer shall take charge of and be responsible for money, resulting from any entertainment that is to be given for the benefit of the Athletic Associations.

ARTICLE VII.

Sec. I. It shall be the duty of the Executive Committee, to decide all questions pertaining to the use of the Athletic Grounds on any particular date.

Sec. II. The Executive Committee shall, after consultation with the Graduate Advisory Committee, decide upon all questions pertaining to the appointment and payment of a trainer.

Sec. III. The Executive Committee shall decide the amount to be contributed by each Association towards the expenses of the Executive

Committee, which expenses shall include the rent and care of the Athletic Grounds, the salaries of the Trainer and Keeper, etc.

SEC. IV. The Executive Committee shall decide all questions, financial or otherwise, which arise between the various organizations.

SEC. V. The Executive Committee shall settle all questions, pertaining to any or all the athletic organizations represented, which are not provided for in the constitutions of those organizations.

SEC. VI. It shall be the duty of the Executive Committee to consult the Graduate Advisory Committee on all questions of importance, pertaining to the general welfare of the College athletics.

SEC. VII. It shall be the duty of the Executive Committee to elect the members of the Graduate Advisory Committee subject to the ratification of the College at its Annual Foot Ball Meeting the first Wednesday in March.

FOOT BALL ASSOCIATION.

ARTICLE I.

This Association shall be known as the Princeton University Foot Ball Association.

ARTICLE II.

Every undergraduate of the College shall be considered a member of this Association.

ARTICLE III.

The Directors of this Association shall consist of the President, Treasurer and Captain. The President to be chosen from the Junior Class, the Treasurer from the Sophomore Class.

ARTICLE IV.

Sec. I. The President and Treasurer shall be elected by a majority vote of those present at the annual Foot Ball Mass Meeting.

Sec. II. The annual Foot Ball Mass Meeting shall take place on the first Wednesday in March and shall be announced in the previous issue of THE PRINCETONIAN and in the Class Rooms.

Sec. III. The officers thus elected shall go into office immediately after Easter.

SEC. IV. No member of team or substitute shall hold the office of President or Treasurer.

ARTICLE V.

SEC. I. Not earlier than ten days after the close of the Foot Ball season, the Captain shall be elected by all the members of the team who played in any of the championship games.

SEC. II. It shall take a majority of all those who are entitled to a vote to elect a Captain.

SEC. III. In case of a tie the President shall cast the deciding vote.

SEC. IV. Any person entitled to a vote for Captain, who is not able to be present, shall have the right to send his vote in writing. Unless said vote be written and signed by the voter, it shall be void.

SEC. V. The election of a Captain shall not be valid until ratified by the Graduate Advisory Committee.

SEC. VI. In case the Graduate Advisory Committee veto his election, or in case the Captain resigns or does not return to College, a Captain shall be elected at the earliest possible date by the members of the team of the previous year, non-resident members voting by proxy.

Article VI.

Sec. I. The duties of the Directors shall be to carry on the business of the Association, arrange games, &c., and to represent the college at all Inter-collegiate Foot Ball Conventions.

Sec. II. It shall be the duty of the Officers to consult the Graduate Advisory Committee on all matters of importance which pertain to the Athletic welfare of the College, such as business of conventions, schedules of games, trainer, &c., and to represent the Association in the Executive Committee.

Article VII.

The duties of the President shall be to preside at all meetings of the Association and the team. He shall carry on all correspondence of the Association, shall keep one copy of all letters written for the Association and shall also keep on file all letters received.

Article VIII.

Sec. I. The duties of the Treasurer shall be to take charge of all moneys, keep a strict account of all expenditures and receipts by the use of an order book and as soon as practicable after each foot ball season, make a report of the same to be published in THE PRINCETONIAN. He shall make a report two weeks before each regular meeting of the University Athletic Association to the University Treasurer concerning the affairs of the Association. He shall also take charge of all suits and foot balls belonging to the Association.

SEC. II. After the close of the Foot Ball season, the Treasurer shall reserve money sufficient to meet all liabilities of the Association, and furthermore an amount sufficient to start in the coming season with. All moneys in the treasury over and above these amounts he shall pay to the Finance Committee to be invested by them for the general athletic interests of the College.

ARTICLE IX.

It shall be the duty of the Captain to choose the team. He shall have absolute power in management of the team on the field. He shall be a delegate to all Inter-Collegiate Foot Ball Conventions.

ARTICLE X.

At the request of thirty men, ten from each of three classes, a meeting shall be called by the President of the Association.

Article XI.

It shall require a majority vote of all the members of the Association to alter or amend in any way their constitution.

BASE BALL ASSOCIATION.

ARTICLE I.

This Association shall be known as the Princeton University Base Ball Association.

ARTICLE II.

Every undergraduate of the College shall be considered a member of this Association.

ARTICLE III.

The Directors of this Association shall consist of the President, Treasurer and Captain. The President to be chosen from the Senior Class, the Treasurer from the Junior Class.

ARTICLE IV.

The Captain shall be elected at the close of the base ball season by all the members of the team who played in any of the championship games.

ARTICLE V.

SEC. I. It shall take a majority of all those who are entitled to vote to elect a Captain.

Sec. II. In case of a tie the President shall cast the deciding vote.

Sec. III. Any person entitled to a veto for Captain who is not able to be present shall have the right to send his vote in writing. Unless said vote be written and signed by the voter, it shall be void.

Sec. IV. The election of a Captain shall not be valid until ratified by the Graduate Advisory Committee.

Sec. V. In case the Graduate Advisory Committee veto his election, or in case the Captain resigns or does not return to College, a Captain shall be elected at the earliest possible date by the members of the team of the previous year; non-resident members voting by proxy.

Article VI.

Sec. I. The President and Treasurer shall be chosen by the College at a mass meeting for that purpose.

Sec. II. The election shall take place on the last Thursday in May.

Sec. III. The officers thus elected shall go into office at the beginning of first term.

Sec. IV. No members of team or substitute shall hold the office of President or Treasurer.

Article VII.

Sec. I. The duties of the Directors shall be to carry on the business of the Association, arrange games, etc.

Sec. II. It shall be the duty of the Directors to consult the Graduate Advisory Committee on all matters of importance which pertain to the welfare of the Association, such as conventions, schedules of games, trainer, etc., and to represent the Association in the Executive Committee.

Article VIII.

The duties of the President shall be to preside at all meetings of the Association and of the club. He shall carry on all correspondence of the Association, shall keep copies of all letters written for the Association and shall keep on file all letters received. He shall be a delegate to all Inter-Collegiate Base Ball Conventions.

Article IX.

Sec. I. The duties of the Treasurer shall be to take charge of all moneys, keep a strict account of all expenditures and receipts by the use of an order book and make at the end of each base ball season, a report of the same to be published in "The Princetonian." He shall make a report two weeks before each regular meeting of the

University Athletic Association to the University Treasurer concerning the affairs of the Association. He shall also take charge of all suits, bats, balls, etc., belonging to the Association.

SEC. II. After the close of the Base Ball season, the Treasurer shall reserve money sufficient to meet all liabilities of the Association, and furthermore an amount sufficient to start in the coming season with. All moneys in the treasury over and above these amounts, he shall pay to the Finance Committee to be invested by them for the general athletic interest of the College.

ARTICLE X.

It shall be the duty of the Captain to choose the team. He shall have absolute power in management of the team on the field. He shall be a delegate to all Inter-Collegiate Base Ball Conventions.

ARTICLE XI.

At the request of thirty men, ten from each of three classes, a meeting shall be called by the President of the Association.

ARTICLE XII.

It shall require a majority vote of all the members of the Association to alter or amend in any way their constitution.

PRINCETON UNIVERSITY TRACK ATHLETIC ASSOCIATION.

ARTICLE I.

This Association shall be known as the Princeton University Track Athletic Association.

ARTICLE II.

Every undergraduate of the college shall be considered a member of this Association.

ARTICLE III.

The officers of this Association shall be a President, chosen from the Senior Class, and a Treasurer, chosen from the Junior Class.

ARTICLE IV.

SEC. I. The President and Treasurer shall be elected by a majority vote of the members present at the annual Mass Meeting of the Association, to be held on the first Wednesday after the Inter-Collegiate games.

SEC. II. The officers thus elected shall go into office at the beginning of the following college year.

Article V.

Sec. I. The Captain shall be elected immediately after the Inter-Collegiate games, by a majority vote of the members of the team competing at such games.

Sec. II. In case of a tie the President shall cast the deciding vote.

Sec. III. Any person entitled to a vote for Captain, who is not able to be present, shall have the right to send his vote in writing. Unless said vote be written and signed by the voter, it shall be void.

Sec. IV. The election of a Captain shall not be valid until ratified by the Graduate Advisory Committee.

Sec. V. In case the Advisory Committee veto his election, or in case the Captain resigns, or does not return to college, a Captain shall be elected at the earliest possible date, by the members of the team.

Article VI.

The Directors shall consist of the President, Treasurer, and Captain.

Article VII.

Sec. I. It shall be the duty of the President to preside at all meetings of the Association. He shall carry on all correspondence, keep copies of all letters written for the Association, and keep on file all letters received.

Sec. II. The duties of the Treasurer shall be to take charge of all moneys, keep a strict account of all receipts and expenditures, and, two weeks before each regular meeting of the University Athletic Association, make a report to the University Treasurer.

Article VIII.

Sec. I. The duties of the Captain shall be to exercise control over the athletic team which shall be chosen by the Directors.

Sec. II. The duties of the Directors shall be to have general control over matters pertaining to the welfare of the Association.

Sec. III. The Directors shall consult the Graduate Advisory Committee on all matters of importance connected with the management of the Association.

Article IX.

Sec. I. There shall be four regular field meetings of the Association during the year. First, Fall Handicap Games some time before Nov. 1st ; Second, Winter Sports in the Gymnasium, on

Washington's Birthday; Third, Spring Open
Handicap Games, at least two weeks before the
I. C. Field Meeting; and Fourth, Class Championship Games for the Peace Cup, some time
during Commencement week.

Sec. II. The rules governing all meetings
shall be those of the Inter-Collegiate Athletic
Association.

Article X.

The delegates to the Inter-Collegiate Convention shall be the President, Treasurer and Captain.

Article XI.

It shall require a majority vote of all the
members of the Association to alter or amend
this Constitution.